# Thoughts

A collection of poems

Lebogang Botlhoko

**ISBN: 978-93-91103-85-9**
**eISBN: 978-93-91103-88-0**



**Publisher**: **Pharos Books (P) Ltd.**
Plot No.-55, Main Mother Dairy Road
Pandav Nagar, East Delhi-110092
**Phone**: +14049995474
**WhatsApp:** +14049995474
**E-mail**: sales@pharosbooks.in
**Website**: www.pharosbooks.in
**Edition:** 2021

**Thoughts**
**Lebogang Botlhoko**

# Contents

# About the Author

Lebogang Botlhoko is a young poet who lives in Gaborone, Botswana. She began writing poetry in 2016 when she was sent off to a boarding school. As she began high school education, she faced some difficulties which became the inspiration behind her writing.

Some have said she is forming art from chaos. She engages in poetry about mental health, love, femininity and healing. She tries to use her poetry to portray how life is a constant rollercoaster but there is still beauty in all the destruction.

# About the Book

The book *Thoughts* is an anthology of poems about the thoughts of a person battling with mental illness.

It explores the complexities, twists and turns of recovery and healing. It serves as a medium for readers to understand that even during the darkest times, light still exists and they are that light.

# Acknowledgements

I would firstly like to thank my mother Tebogo Botlhoko and my father Daniel Botlhoko for continuosly reminding me that broken crayons can still colour. I have also been blessed with paternal parents whose hands have been extended to me when I felt I had nowhere to go and for that I will be eternaly grateful.

To all my friends, thank you for believing in me when I didn't believe in myself. The simple words "thank you" would pale and diminish in the sheer enormity of the gratitude I owe.

# In the beginning

Sometimes I stare at people mindlessly
Watching them go about their lives
Wondering what could be wrong
Wondering what could be right
We all hold a different story

## After reading her death note

Oh darling,
You were never ugly, society is
You were in fact a piece of art waiting to be splashed with colour
And you died while waiting
I told you that your imperfections made you beautiful
I wish you really knew what I meant
I watched as your torturous thoughts
Slowly dragged you into your grave
Slowly turning you into dust
They never mourned for you Because they long saw your saddened death.

# Lost soul

She's just a lost soul
A soul wandering around searching for happiness,

True happiness

She wonders when, how she turned to this
She was once a happy seven year old
Now she's a broken, shuttered teenager
She misses those days

Those days when all she thought of,
was being happy

Now all she thinks about is sadness,
Pain is her drug and she's addicted
She inflicts the pain on herself
Her thoughts will be the cause of her death
Maybe, then they will notice
Maybe then they will miss her,

Miss her when she's gone.

# When you ask

When you ask to know more about me
Tell me which part you want to know about
My heart has broken into so many pieces
So you need to decide which story,
you want to know about
And how the broken piece of me,
disintegrated and broke
Into the nothingness that I am now.

## Can't you see

Can't you see mum?
That the life you've given me is killing me.

## Disappointment

This is it, my demise I thought to myself
Woke up on a hospital bed days after.

# Self harm

And that was when I knew
how it felt to be empty
But yearn to feel something,
Anything
That was how it all began
A little emptiness.

# Red lines on brown lines

I almost forgot how it felt
Goddamn it, the sting
How could I ever forget?

# Some things are not worth the trouble

I scream and shout to make the
Voices go away but they have
Held me captive again
I'm a prisoner in my own mind
Bound by chains and voices that just
Won't let me go
I have been sealed by a great rock
To this life
And sometimes I don't think
I want to break free.

# Shattering

On rare days, when the thoughts
Get the best of me,
I begin to carve the words
that I believe are true On my skin
"Failure, fat, not good enough"
I carve them slowly and when the blood
Stains are all over my sheets
I'm reminded that
"Everything beautiful has a consequence"
On other days I want to cut to the bone
I want to skin myself alive
And kill this body
because it has brought misery
I want to take this platter life has given me
And smash it on the floor
till it breaks into a million pieces
The even more million pieces
that it broke me into
I don't want this body anymore
I don't want this anymore
I'm not sure I can keep it much longer
I am tired
The type of tired that two days
of sleep cannot fix

The type of tired that eats
at my bones each day
The tired, that I cannot talk about because
I don't want to come off as asking
for pity or pitying myself
Because that's what people mistake
being sad for
But this sadness, it's the one that kills you
The sadness that takes so much
of you along with it
This deep, paralyzing sadness
will turn you into a Lazarus
If no one can take this Lazarus of my body
and put it to rest,
I will.

# I want

I want to be a cloud
So I linger in the air with no emotion,
So I cry when I have had enough.

# Feelings

Feelings of wondrous infatuation
Lingering in the air,
I hate that it's temporary.

# Since I

Since I met you,
I've started wishing for more time
I want more time with you.

## Yours Sincerely

I think losing you would hurt
More than any immense hurt
I have ever felt before
You have become such a huge
part of my life and trust me
When I say I don't want to see
a world without you
A world without you would be dull
I want to wake up and see pink swirls
Instead of a grey sky
You're the person my heart goes out to
This love for you, it grows and grows
And I think with time it will implode
You are the sweet, pure love
my grandma spoke about
You are that sweet honey
that my gran loved so dearly
The honey, it came from bees
that hurt and sting
But it turned out to be sweet
The bees represent what you've been
through
And the honey is the outcome
It truly is admirable how you carry yourself

despite everything
The true beauty is in how you are kind
in an unkind world
It is in the way you're still able to see a little
bit of beauty in the world
Your life is your canvas,
Paint on it however you wish to
I've given you the paint brushes to do so
Paint till it all looks beautiful
I know that you'll see the beauty in it too
As you begin to paint, you may not see it
but in the end you will
You may not see the beauty in yourself,
the perfection that I see
But you will as you continue to paint
your canvas
I love everything you hate about yourself.

## Like the sun

Like the sun,
I will rise and fall and rise again.

## What we had

What we had is what I'd like to call
Collateral beauty
So beautiful and yet so damaging
I'm not romanticizing the toxicity,
I'm simply acknowledging that happiness
does exist in a tragedy
You have made a home in the deepest,
desolate parts
Of my heart and now,
A home in my dreams
You are a tenant who refuses to be evicted.

# Maybe I'm paying

Maybe I'm paying for the sins of my past self
Paying for the hearts I held in my hands
And crushed like they were of no significance
I must be paying for the tears
you shed after the best
I thought I could do for you was leave
I must be paying in seven fold.

## Dear Uncle

You taught me many things but not how to
be a poet in an undelightful world
You taught me how to love but you forgot
To tell me about the pain that comes
with unrequited love
You taught me kindness, but you forgot
To tell me that not everyone
would be kind to me
You taught and showed me
beautiful things but
You forgot to tell me
that not all that glitters is gold

Dear uncle,
you took out of me a piece when you left
A piece that can never be returned,
A piece that is buried rather eight feet deep
along with your body and soul
Dear uncle,
your teachings have both made
and broken me
It's been years but my mind
can't stop tracing back to the memories
made

The songs we sang and learnt together,
The peace that emerged in your presence
But then, I came to a realisation
that it solves nothing
Wondering what could have been done
solves nothing
I further learnt that we have to choose
who we want to be
And not let the situation choose us
I used to read a quotation that said
"Soon when all is well, you will look back on
this day and thank God you never gave up"
This is it, the terrific day.

# You can

Control what you can
When everything feels out of control.

# I never knew

I never knew what they meant
when they said soulmates
Were not always found in relationships
I thought that surely my soulmate
would have to be
Someone I get to marry

My soulmate would have to be someone
I spend the rest of my life with
in holy matrimony
But you came into my life and helped me
see through
This window I was so terrified
of looking through,

Through this lense
I was so scared of using
My favourite writer once said
"You are so busy being you that you have no
idea how utterly unprecedented you are"

Dear Soulmate
"You are so busy being you that you have no
idea how utterly unprecedented you are"
You give me premature
ventricular contractions
You make my heart skip a beat
My soulmate

You are the epitome of beauty
The epitome of love
The epitome of long lasting
You are the epitome of greatness
You my dear, are going to change the world
My soulmate
I think I've wished for you before, on the
days I wanted somebody who would hold me
When I couldn't hold myself
Somebody who could see my flaws and still
think I'm beautiful
Somebody who would stay

The only problem is I went looking
in all the wrong places
I was so clouded with the idea that my
soulmate had to be my lover
And yet, you were standing right
in front of me
My soulmate
There were days when I could not
bear being alive
But you told me to rumble or simply
type away
Then go through the texts another time to
Pick some things to form art
from the destruction
This is me forming art from the destruction
My soulmate,

I am immensely in love with each
and every part of your being
My soulmate.

# I was told

I was told that when he gets too close
I must run in hopes of finding humanity
I must run in hopes of finding someone
Who will make me feel the slightest bit of safe
In a world so cruel.

# I am angry

I am angry,
I am angry for my sisters who walk around
wondering if they will be next
I am angry, angry for my sisters who walk
around with emptiness in their bodies,
emptiness in their souls
I am angry, I am mad because
my sisters are scared
My sisters are scarred
I am angry because men keep trying to
justify their actions by saying
"She asked for it"
Well, I am saying this loud and clear
I am angry, I am big mad
Because I continue to see my sisters crumble
I continue to see my brothers crumble too
We wine and dine with rapists every day
We laugh and smile with predators every day
Just tell me, siyaphi, rea kae, re tshepa mang?
Words cannot express my rage
I cannot begin to fathom why people can be so ruthless
If only we saw souls instead of bodies,
how different our world would be
I am angry, I am mad

Because humanity is perishing,
humanity is diminishing
I hate that the rapists become
the victims in society's eyes
Because "she was dressed in
a provoking manner"
I am angry because young girls are taught
how to not get raped
Instead of boys being taught not to rape
From a tender age, boys are told to
"go get the girls"
And when they don't, it turns into force
It turns into rape
I am mad because men feel entitled
I am big mad because I am the
one who cries myself to sleep
I am big mad because I'm the
one who is hurting
I am big mad for my sisters.

# As a female

As a female living in this day and now
I have been made to adjust to the filthy system
Why do I have to wear a long skirt in order
Not to provoke men who simply cannot
control themselves
Why is it that when I'm walking in the dark,
I'm "asking for danger", "calling for rape"
or perhaps "asking for it"
Tell me why I must live my life
on the assumption that
Grown men with brains, like myself
cannot see the
Contrast between right and wrong,
consent and dissent
Tell me why I must live my life in fear
because
He cannot respect myself and himself
Enough to leave me alone
For years, women have been made
to wrap around a man's finger
Because he is a man and has male genitals
that he simply cannot control
I must look "decent"
But you see, there is no justification

for that anymore
I have seen women draped in clothing
get raped
I have seen men rape babies but still they
want to blame it on the women
"Dress properly, cover up those thighs" they
say, "You are making me uncomfortable"
Tell me why this has been normalised
Why must I live in fear, wrapped
around his finger
Why must I be in a position of violation?
Why must I live the rest of my life mistaking
the good men for the bad,
Mistaking their actions for yours
I have built a strong wall of boundaries
only for my wall
To be kicked and destroyed by a man who
does not have his own boundaries
I learnt to be shrewd in this world and yet
my dignity is taken in a split two seconds
I am like a puppet whose strings
have snapped,
How horrifying.

# Learning

I am learning that self-love is not conditional
Even on the days I feel blue and small,
I am magical
I am learning to forgive.
Even without an apology,
I want to put this out there.
I forgive you.

# Letter to the broken

I know life may kick you to the curb
It may feel like the walls of the world
are closing in on you
It may seem the whole world is out to get
you
But all you need to know is that you are
The light of your own tunnel
Switch yourself on
And venture this secretive beauty.

# Lament to this

Lament to this body I call my own
The body I have never been
to call my own till this day
I destroyed you for a peace of mind
I did not get
No one ever taught me how to apologise
to my own body
How do I make amends with someone
I spent half my lifetime trying to break
For so long, I was so angry because I had a
disease that convinced me
I was better off dead
Because no one likes messy
I overheard a conversation
"Why would such a beautiful person
want to die?" He said
"Because life hasn't been so beautiful
to "me was her response"
But today I want to say
Body, I am sorry
I'm not going to punish you for trying
so hard to keep me alive anymore
I will not make you a slave to my mind
I am here to make amends, I come in peace

I am here to tell those terrible thoughts that
there is no room anymore
I am finally stopping the calculator
in my head,
I am feeding you
I will take all the love I have in my heart
and give it to you
I will not degrade you into smallness
I will let you take up space
I will let your presence be known
I will celebrate your existence
I will remind you every day that
you are enchanted,
You are special
And you are beautiful
That the world is your oyster
Broken crayons still colour,
My love.

# Woman

As females of the twenty first century
Or may I say the "doomed century"
We have let the male population
make us feel little and inferior
They have hurt us and often times,
we mistook it for love
Making us their puppets as they pulled
the strings
They have made us feel so small that
Sometimes we forget the power and magic
we carry within ourselves
We carry the weight of the world and yet we
still live on and anticipate the next day
We have the power to build
a home from nothing
The power to build love into the same males
that turn against us like we are nothing
This is a letter to the women who doubt
their abilities and capabilities
This is a letter to the women,
The women who place their value
in the words he says
And how much he drools over your body
Your body is enchanted and you

are dripping honey
Oh lady, this is a letter to you
To you who cries herself to sleep because he
could not realise your worth
You are power and magic in one
Lady, don't do that to yourself
Don't do that to yourself
Don't do that to yourself
Can't you see the world is made of you and
You are made of the world
Woman!

# You are

You are a diamond
But why do you let them treat you like glass.

## You have

You have shown me
That people can be great and still crumble.

# I hope

I hope you find hope in my eyes,
Dear one.

# On the days

And on the days you feel the worst,
Remember you are infinitely
loved by someone who sees
Galaxies in you when you see an empty sky
On the days you feel down and out
Remember you are very deeply
loved by someone
Who talks to God about you and is
constantly rooting for you.

# Even if

Even if breathing becomes
the only thing you are doing, Keep doing it.

# I know

I know we all have reasons
why we choose the knife
But please don't die
Put down that razor, don't end your fight
You can't have fought this hard
to lose the war.

# And if

And if you don't want to talk about it
I can sit in the dark with you
Just so you don't feel alone.

# Expressing emotion

Expressing your emotions
Shouldn't make you feel so small
You deserve more than that, my dear.

# Forever thank

I will forever thank the universe
For letting me meet someone
profound as you are.

# Daughter

When I have a daughter,
I will teach her that her body is hers
And hers to be loved
I will teach her that loving herself
Will move mountains
That self-love should be a superpower
she must possess.

## You must know

You must know,
I love all the parts about you
That you despise the most
You deserve all the love you keep
giving the world.

# The moon is beautiful

This is a love letter from me to you
A book that inspires others
may not always inspire you,
I hope, in my hands,
you have found it at long last.
Thank you for accepting the invitation
into my mind and heart
It has been an honour having you as a guest
Someone instead of saying "I love you"
Said "the moon is beautiful"
And that has stuck with me since
To my dear reader,
The moon is beautiful.

## 'Til the end

And her
Tears are ashes
Of misery.

www.ingramcontent.com/pod-product-compliance
Ingram Content Group UK Ltd.
Pitfield, Milton Keynes, MK11 3LW, UK
UKHW022007190726
13853UKWH00004B/1792